A LITTLE PRINCESS

Ralph Crewe lives in India, with his little daughter Sara. He is a rich man, and when he brings Sara to Miss Minchin's school in London, Miss Minchin is very pleased. She likes girls with rich fathers, because it is good for her school. Mr Crewe loves Sara very much, and he buys her lots of beautiful dresses, and books, and dolls. Miss Minchin smiles, but she says to her sister: 'Sara looks like a little princess, not a schoolgirl!'

Mr Crewe goes back to his work in India, and Sara begins her new life at school. She is a kind, friendly girl. Everybody likes her, and she soon makes friends.

But when you are rich, everybody is your friend. On Sara's eleventh birthday, there is some terrible news from India. Poor Sara is very unhappy, and she quickly learns who her true friends are . . .

OXFORD BOOKWORMS LIBRARY

Human Interest

A Little Princess

Stage 1 (400 headwords)

Series Editor: Jennifer Bassett
Founder Editor: Tricia Hedge
Activities Editors: Jennifer Bassett and Alison Baxter

FRANCES HODGSON BURNETT

A Little Princess

Retold by
Jennifer Bassett

Illustrated by
Gwen Tourret

OXFORD UNIVERSITY PRESS

OXFORD
UNIVERSITY PRESS

Great Clarendon Street, Oxford OX2 6DP

Oxford University Press is a department of the University of Oxford.
It furthers the University's objective of excellence in research, scholarship,
and education by publishing worldwide in

Oxford New York

Auckland Cape Town Dar es Salaam Hong Kong Karachi
Kuala Lumpur Madrid Melbourne Mexico City Nairobi
New Delhi Shanghai Taipei Toronto

With offices in

Argentina Austria Brazil Chile Czech Republic France Greece
Guatemala Hungary Italy Japan Poland Portugal Singapore
South Korea Switzerland Thailand Turkey Ukraine Vietnam

OXFORD and OXFORD ENGLISH are registered trade marks of
Oxford University Press in the UK and in certain other countries

This simplified edition © Oxford University Press 2008

Database right Oxford University Press (maker)

First published in Oxford Bookworms 1998

20

ISBN 978 0 19 478906 6

A complete recording of this Bookworms edition of
A Little Princess is available.

Printed in China

Word count (main text): 5840 words

For more information on the Oxford Bookworms Library,
visit www.oup.com/elt/gradedreaders

CONTENTS

STORY INTRODUCTION   i

1 School in England   1
2 The diamond mines   8
3 The new servant-girl   16
4 Ram Dass and the monkey   22
5 The magic   30
6 Lost and found   37

GLOSSARY   42
ACTIVITIES: Before Reading   44
ACTIVITIES: While Reading   45
ACTIVITIES: After Reading   48
ABOUT THE AUTHOR   52
ABOUT THE BOOKWORMS LIBRARY   53

1
School in England

One cold winter day a little girl and her father arrived in London. Sara Crewe was seven years old, and she had long black hair and green eyes. She sat in the cab next to her father and looked out of the window at the tall houses and the dark sky.

'What are you thinking about, Sara?' Mr Crewe asked.

'What are you thinking about, Sara?' Mr Crewe asked.

'You are very quiet.' He put his arm round his daughter.

'I'm thinking about our house in India,' said Sara. 'And the hot sun and the blue sky. I don't think I like England very much, Father.'

'Yes, it's very different from India,' her father said. 'But you must go to school in London, and I must go back to India and work.'

'Yes, Father, I know,' said Sara. 'But I want to be with you. Please come to school with me! I can help you with your lessons.'

Mr Crewe smiled, but he was not happy. He loved his little Sara very much, and he did not want to be without her. Sara's mother was dead, and Sara was his only child. Father and daughter were very good friends.

Soon they arrived at Miss Minchin's School for Girls and went into the big house.

Miss Minchin was a tall woman in a black dress. She looked at Sara, and then gave a very big smile.

'What a beautiful child!' she said to Mr Crewe.

Sara stood quietly and watched Miss Minchin. 'Why does she say that?' she thought. 'I am not beautiful, so why does she say it?'

Sara was not beautiful, but her father was rich. And Miss Minchin liked girls with rich fathers, because it was good for the school (and good for Miss Minchin, too).

'Sara is a good girl,' Mr Crewe said to Miss Minchin.

Miss Minchin was a tall woman in a black dress.

'Her mother was French, so she speaks French well. She loves books, and she reads all the time. But she must play with the other girls and make new friends, too.'

'Of course,' said Miss Minchin. She smiled again. 'Sara is going to be very happy here, Mr Crewe.'

3

Mr Crewe stayed in London for a week. He and Sara went to the shops, and he bought many beautiful, expensive dresses for his daughter. He bought books, and flowers for her room, and a big doll with beautiful dresses, too.

Miss Minchin smiled, but she said to her sister Amelia: 'All that money on dresses for a child of seven! She looks like a little princess, not a schoolgirl!'

Mr Crewe bought many expensive dresses for his daughter.

When Mr Crewe left London, he was very sad. Sara was very sad too, but she did not cry. She sat in her room and thought about her father on the ship back to India.

'Father wants me to be happy,' she said to her new doll. 'I love him very much and I want to be a good daughter, so I must be happy.'

It was a very big, and very beautiful doll, but of course it could not answer.

It was a big, beautiful doll.

Sara soon made new friends in the school. Some little rich girls are not very nice children – they think they are important because they have money and lots of expensive things. But Sara was different. She liked beautiful dresses and dolls, but she was more interested in people, and books, and telling stories.

She was very good at telling stories. She was a clever child, and the other girls loved to listen to her. The

The stories were all about kings and queens and princesses.

stories were all about kings and queens and princesses and wonderful countries across the sea.

'How do you think of all those things?' asked her best friend, Ermengarde.

'I have all these pictures in my head,' said Sara. 'So it's easy to tell stories about them.'

Poor Ermengarde was not clever. She could never remember any of her school lessons, and Miss Minchin was always angry with her.

Sara often helped Ermengarde with her lessons. 'Listen, Ermie,' she said. 'You remember that French king, Louis the Sixteenth? Well, this is a story about him. One day in 1792 …'

6

And so Ermengarde learnt her lessons through Sara's stories, and she loved her friend very much. But not everybody was Sara's friend. Lavinia was an older girl. Before Sara came, Lavinia was the richest and the most important girl in the school. But Sara's father was richer than Lavinia's father. So now Sara was more important than Lavinia, and Lavinia did not like that.

'Oh, Sara is *so* clever!' Lavinia often said. 'Sara is *so* good at French! Her dresses are *so* beautiful, and she can sing *so* well! And she is *so* rich! Of course Miss Minchin likes her best!'

Sara did not answer when Lavinia said these things. Sometimes, it was not easy, but Sara was a kind, friendly girl, and she did not like to be angry with anyone.

Now Sara was important, and Lavinia did not like that.

2
The diamond mines

♢ ♢ ♢

And so three years went by. Sara's father wrote
to her often, and Sara wrote loving little letters
back to him. One day a very exciting letter arrived.
Everybody in the school talked about it for days.

'*My friend,*' wrote Mr Crewe, '*has some mines in
northern India, and a month ago his workers found
diamonds there. There are thousands of diamonds in*

'*There are thousands of diamonds in these mines . . .*'

8

these mines, but it is expensive work to get them out. My friend needs my help. So, Little Missus' (this was Mr Crewe's special name for Sara), *'I am putting all my money into my friend's diamond mines, and one day you and I are going to be very rich ...'*

Sara was not interested in money, but a story about diamond mines in India was exciting. Nearly everybody was very pleased for Sara, but not Lavinia, of course.

'Huh!' she said. 'My mother has a diamond. Lots of people have diamonds. What's so interesting about diamond mines?'

'But there are thousands of diamonds in these mines,' said Ermengarde. 'Perhaps millions of them!'

Lavinia laughed. 'Is Sara going to wear diamonds in her hair at breakfast, then? Or is it "Princess Sara" now?'

Sara's face went red. She looked at Lavinia angrily, but said quietly, 'Some people call me "princess". I know that. But princesses don't get angry or say unkind things, so I'm not going to say anything to you, Lavinia.'

'To me, you *are* a princess,' Ermengarde said to Sara later. 'And you always look like a princess, in your beautiful dresses.'

'*My mother has a diamond.*'

9

Sara was a princess to another girl, too. This was Becky. She was a servant in Miss Minchin's school, and she was only fourteen years old, but she worked all day and sometimes half the night. She carried things upstairs and downstairs, she cleaned the floors, she made the fires, and she was always tired and hungry and dirty. She and Sara had very different lives.

Becky cleaned the floors, made the fires . . .

But one day Sara came into her bedroom, and there was Becky, sleeping in a chair.

'Oh, you poor thing!' Sara said.

Then Becky opened her eyes and saw Sara. She got up at once. 'Oh, Miss!' she said. 'I'm very sorry, Miss! I just sat down for a minute and—'

'Don't be afraid,' said Sara. She gave Becky a friendly smile. 'You were tired. That's all.'

There was Becky, sleeping in a chair.

'Are you – are you going to tell Miss Minchin?' asked Becky. She began to move to the door.

'Of course not,' said Sara. 'Please don't run away. Sit down again for a minute. You look so tired.'

'Oh, Miss, I can't!' Becky said. 'You're very kind, Miss, but Miss Minchin—'

'Please,' said Sara. She took Becky's hand. 'You're only a little girl, like me. Let's be friends.'

And so Becky sat down again, and soon she and Sara were friends. Nobody knew about this, of course. Rich little girls at Miss Minchin's school did not make friends with servant-girls, and it was a wonderful thing for

Becky. Nearly every day she and Sara met in Sara's
bedroom, just for five or ten minutes. Becky was always
hungry, and Sara often bought nice things for her to eat.
They sat and talked, and sometimes Sara told Becky
some of her stories. Becky loved that.

'Oh, Miss,' she said. 'You tell them so beautifully!
Sometimes I like your stories better than things to eat.'

And after those visits to Sara's room, Becky always
felt better – not so tired, and not so hungry.

Some months later Sara had her eleventh birthday.
Lessons stopped for the afternoon and there was a big
party for all the girls in the school.

Everybody at Sara's party was very happy.

12

'This party is expensive for us,' Miss Minchin said to her sister Amelia. 'But it looks good for the school.'

That afternoon there was a visitor to the school – Miss Minchin's lawyer. He went with Miss Minchin into her office and they closed the door. In the schoolroom next door there was a lot of noise from Sara's party. Everybody in there was very happy.

But in the office Miss Minchin was not happy. She looked at the lawyer angrily. 'What are you saying? Mr Crewe has no money? What about the diamond mines?'

'There are *no* diamond mines,' said the lawyer. 'Well, there are mines, but there are no diamonds in them.'

'But Mr Crewe's good friend—' began Miss Minchin.

'Mr Crewe's good friend,' said the lawyer, 'ran away with all Mr Crewe's money. Ralph Crewe was ill with a fever, and when he heard about this, he got worse. A week later he was dead.'

'Dead!' cried Miss Minchin. 'But what about his daughter Sara? And this expensive birthday party?'

'Sara Crewe has no money,' said the lawyer. 'Not a penny in the world, Miss Minchin. Not a penny.'

'She must leave my school at once,' Miss Minchin said angrily. 'She must go this afternoon!'

'Where?' said the lawyer. 'Out into the streets? An eleven-year-old girl? That's not going to look very good for your school, Miss Minchin.'

Miss Minchin's face went red.

'You can't put her out in the streets,' said the lawyer. He stood up. 'But perhaps she can work for you.'

The lawyer left, and Miss Minchin called her sister Amelia. 'Bring Sara Crewe here at once,' she said.

Two minutes later Sara, in her beautiful blue party dress, stood in front of Miss Minchin.

'Have you a black dress, Sara?' Miss Minchin said coldly.

'Yes, Miss Minchin,' said Sara. 'But it's very small.'

'She must leave my school at once,' Miss Minchin said.

'Go and put it on at once,' said Miss Minchin. 'Your father is dead. There were no diamond mines, and your father's friend ran away with all his money. You have nothing. Not a penny. But I am going to be very kind to you. You can stay in my house, but now you must be a servant and work for your bread. You can sleep in a servant's room upstairs, next to Becky's room.'

3
The new servant-girl

♦ ♦ ♦

That evening, in the little attic room, Sara sat on the bed in her old black dress. She did not cry, but her face was white and she did not move or speak for hours.

Late at night the door opened quietly, and Becky looked in. Her eyes were red from crying. 'Oh, Miss,' she said. 'All the servants are talking about it. I'm so sorry – so sorry!' She looked at Sara's white face, and began to cry again. Then she ran to Sara, and took her hand.

At last Sara moved. Slowly, she turned her head and looked at Becky. 'Oh, Becky,' she said. And that was all.

Becky ran to Sara, and took her hand.

That first night in the attic was very long. Sara did not sleep. 'Father is dead,' she whispered, again and again. 'Father is dead. I'm never going to see him again.'

The next morning Sara's new life began. She learnt to clean floors and to make fires. She ran upstairs and downstairs, and she worked in the kitchen.

'Run down to the shops and get me some apples.'

The cook was a big woman with a red, angry face. 'So,' she said, 'the little rich girl with the diamond mines is now a servant, eh?' She looked at Sara. 'Now, I'm making apple pies this morning. Run down to the shops and get me some apples. And be quick!'

So Sara ran to the shops, and carried a big bag of apples back to the house. Then she cleaned the kitchen floor, and carried hot water up to all the bedrooms.

She worked every day, from early in the morning to late at night. She helped in the school, too.

'You speak French well,' Miss Minchin said to her coldly. 'So you can teach French to the younger children. But you're only a servant. Don't forget that.'

The first months of Sara's new life were very hard. She was always tired and hungry, but she never cried. At night, in her little attic, she thought about her father, dead in India all those miles away.

'I must be brave,' she said. 'Father always wanted me to be brave. And I have a bed to sleep in, and something to eat every day. Lots of people don't have that.'

At first Sara's only friend was Becky. Every day Becky came into Sara's room. They did not talk much, but it helped Sara a lot to see Becky's friendly, smiling face.

The girls in the school were sorry for Sara, but Sara was a servant now, and they could not be friendly with a servant. Lavinia, of course, was pleased. 'I never liked Sara Crewe,' she told her friends. 'And I was right about the diamonds – there weren't any!'

Ermengarde was very unhappy. When she saw Sara in the school, Sara walked past her and did not speak. Poor Ermengarde loved Sara and wanted to be friendly, but she was not clever, and she did not understand.

One morning, very early, she got quietly out of bed, went upstairs to the attics, and opened Sara's door.

'What are you doing here?' said Sara.

'Ermengarde!' Sara said. 'What are you doing here?'

Ermengarde began to cry. 'Oh, Sara, please tell me. What *is* the matter? Why don't you like me now?'

'I *do* like you,' Sara said. 'Of course I do. But, you see, everything is different now. Miss Minchin doesn't want me to talk to the girls. Most of them don't want to talk to me. And I thought, perhaps, you didn't want to …'

'But I'm your *friend*!' cried Ermengarde. 'I'm *always* going to be your friend – and *nobody* can stop me!'

Sara took Ermengarde's hands. She suddenly felt very happy. Perhaps she cried a little, too. Who can say?

There was only one chair, so the two friends sat on the

bed. Ermengarde looked round the attic. 'Oh, Sara, how can you live in this room? It's so cold and – and dirty.'

'It's not so bad,' said Sara. 'And I've got lots of friends. There's Becky in the next room, and – come and see.'

She moved the table under the window, and then she and Ermengarde stood on it and looked out of the

'Watch,' Sara said.

window, over the roofs of the houses. In her pocket Sara had some small pieces of bread. She put her hand out of the window, with the bread on it. 'Watch,' she said.

After a minute a little brown bird flew down to Sara's hand and began to eat the bread. Then a second bird came, and a third, and a fourth.

'Oh Sara, how wonderful!' said Ermengarde.

'They know I'm their friend,' said Sara, 'so they're not afraid. Sometimes they come into the room, too.'

Ermengarde looked across the roof to the next attic window. 'Who lives in that house?' she asked.

'Nobody,' said Sara sadly. 'So I never see anybody at that window, and I can only talk to the birds.'

But one night, two or three weeks later, Becky came into Sara's room. She was very excited.

'Oooh, Miss!' she said. 'An Indian gentleman is moving into the house next door. Well, he's English, but he lived in India for years and years. And now he's going to live next door. He's very rich, and he's ill. Something bad happened to him, but I don't know what.'

Sara laughed. 'How do you know all this?' she said.

'Well, Miss, you know the Carmichael family across the street?' Becky said. 'I'm friendly with their kitchen-girl, and she told me. Mr Carmichael is the Indian gentleman's lawyer, so they know all about him.'

4
Ram Dass and the monkey

Every morning, when Sara gave the birds their bread, she looked across to the attic window next door. But nobody opened it. Nobody called out 'Good morning!' across the roof, or gave Sara a friendly smile.

'Perhaps the Indian gentleman's servants all sleep downstairs,' she thought sadly.

Her life was very lonely now. She saw Becky every day, of course, but they did not have much time for talking. The cook and the other servants were not friendly. Sometimes, at night, Ermengarde came up to Sara's room, but it was not easy for her to come often.

At the window was a monkey.

Then one evening, Sara was in her attic when she heard a noise on the roof. She looked up – and there at the open window was a small monkey.

'Oh, you dear little thing!' cried Sara.

At once, the monkey jumped down and began to run round the room. Sara laughed. She got up on the table and looked

22

Ram Dass thanked Sara again and again.

out of her window, and at the next window she saw a face – the smiling face of an Indian lascar.

'Oh,' cried Sara, 'have you got a monkey? He's in my room.'

The lascar's name was Ram Dass, and yes, it was his monkey. He gave Sara a big smile.

'I'm so sorry,' he said. 'Can I come and get him?'

'Oh yes, please,' said Sara. 'I think he's afraid of me. And he runs so fast! But can you get across the roof?'

Yes, Ram Dass could, and a minute later he was in Sara's room. Soon the monkey jumped into his arms, and Ram Dass thanked Sara again and again. Then he went away, across the roof, back into the house next door.

◈

Sara went to the shops five or six times a day, and when she walked past the house next door, she often thought about the Indian gentleman. She felt sorry for him. He had no wife or family, and the doctor visited the house every day. Mr Carmichael the lawyer often visited, too, and sometimes the Carmichael children went with him.

Sara was pleased about that. 'It's nice to see friendly faces when you are ill,' she thought.

The Indian gentleman thought that, too. He liked children very much, but he was a very unhappy man. Mr Carmichael was his friend, and he talked to him a lot. But they talked about only one thing.

'I *must* find the child,' said the Indian gentleman (his name was Mr Carrisford). 'I must find her and take care of her. But where is she? Here I am, with all this money from the diamond mines – and half of it is Ralph Crewe's money. Oh, Carmichael, why did I leave my friend and run away when things looked bad? Why?'

'You ran away because you were ill with a fever,' said Mr Carmichael. 'It nearly killed you, remember?'

'And it *did* kill poor Ralph,' said Mr Carrisford. 'He put all his money into the mines because I was his friend. But at first we didn't find any diamonds, and all Ralph's money was gone. I was afraid to tell him, so I ran away. And later, when we *did* find diamonds, Ralph was dead.' He laughed, angrily. 'What a brave friend I was!'

'I must find the child and take care of her.'

'It's not easy to be brave,' Mr Carmichael said quietly, 'when you're ill with a fever.'

Mr Carrisford looked into the fire. 'Ram Dass tells me,' he said, 'about a little servant-girl next door. The monkey ran away, and Ram Dass went across the roof to get him back from her room. The poor child sleeps in a cold, dirty attic, and works about sixteen hours a day. Is Ralph's daughter living like that? I can't stop thinking about it.'

'We're going to find her one day,' said Mr Carmichael.

'But how?' said Mr Carrisford. He put his head in his hands. 'I never saw her. I don't know her name! Ralph always called her his "Little Missus". We talked all the time about the mines. He never told me the name of her school. Her mother was French, so did he take her to a school in France? Or was it in England?'

'Well, we know there was a child at a school in Paris,' said Mr Carmichael, 'with the name of Carew or Crewe. Her father died suddenly, and a Russian family took her away with them, because she was a friend of their daughter. Perhaps this girl is Ralph Crewe's child. Next week I'm going to Moscow to look for her.'

'I want to go with you, but I'm not well,' said Mr Carrisford. 'I must find her, Carmichael. I must. Every night, in my dreams, I see Ralph Crewe's face, and he says: "Tom, Tom, where is my Little Missus?" And I have no answer for him.' Mr Carrisford took his friend's hand. 'Help me to find her. Help me.'

Winter came, with its short, dark days, and the attic rooms were very cold. There were no fires for servant-girls, and often Sara and Becky could not sleep because of the cold. Sara was taller now, and her old black dress was very short. Her shoes were old, and she had no warm coat for the winter weather. She was thin, too. She did not get very much to eat, and she was always hungry.

She carried big baskets of shopping through the rain and the snow. One day she found a sixpence in the snow, and she bought some hot new bread with it. Then she saw a child by the door of the shop. The child had no shoes and no coat, and her thin face was blue with cold.

'She is hungrier than I am,' thought Sara. And she gave her hot new bread to the child.

When she got back to the school, Miss Minchin was angry. 'Cook is waiting for you, Sara. Why are you late?'

'She is hungrier than I am,' thought Sara.

'Oh, here's Princess Sara,' Lavinia said.

'I can't walk quickly through the snow,' said Sara. 'My shoes are old, Miss Minchin, and my feet get very cold.'

Miss Minchin did not like to hear this. 'Don't speak to me like that!' she said. 'I am kind to you, I'm giving you a home, but you never say "thank you" to me.'

Sara looked at her. 'You are *not* kind,' she said quietly. 'And this is *not* a home.'

'Go to your room at once!' said Miss Minchin.

On the stairs Sara met Lavinia. Lavinia looked at her and gave a little laugh. 'Oh, here's Princess Sara,' she said, 'in her old dress and her dirty shoes!'

In the attic, Sara sat down on the chair by her table.

'I must be brave,' she whispered. 'A princess is always

brave, so I must be, too. But it's not easy.' She put her head down on her arms. 'Oh, Father, do you remember your Little Missus? Can you see me now?'

And in the house next door Mr Carrisford sat by a warm fire. Moscow is a long way from London, and he could only wait, but he thought about Ralph Crewe's child every day. He thought about other children, too.

'Ram Dass,' he said. 'How is that poor little servant-girl next door? Can we do something for her?'

'I see her in the street every day,' said Ram Dass. 'In the rain, in the snow. She looks thin and hungry. But we can help her. I can easily get in through her attic window. Listen ...' And he talked for some minutes.

Mr Carrisford smiled. 'Yes,' he said to Ram Dass. 'Yes, I like it. Let's do it.'

'Listen ...' said Ram Dass.

5
The magic

◇ ◇ ◇

One night, a week later, Ermengarde got quietly out of bed and went upstairs to the attic. Sara was not there, so Ermengarde sat on the bed and waited. At ten o'clock Sara came slowly up the stairs and into the room.

Ermengarde looked at her. 'Oh, Sara!' she cried. 'Are you ill? Your face is white, and you look so tired!'

'It was a hard day, Ermie,' said Sara. She sat down. 'Miss Minchin was angry with Cook. Then Cook was angry with us. Becky and I had no dinner and no tea.'

'Does that happen often?' said Ermengarde unhappily. 'You never told me. Are you – are you hungry now?'

Sara looked at her. 'Yes,' she whispered. 'Yes, I am. I would like to eat that table. I would like to eat *you*.'

Ermengarde jumped up. 'Sara,' she cried. 'I had a box of things from home today. There's a big cake in it. I'm going to get it – now! You and Becky can eat it all!'

Soon, Ermengarde was back. The three girls sat

'There's a big cake in it.'

30

on Sara's bed, and there were some happy smiles when Ermengarde opened her box and took out the cake.

'Oh, Miss, look at that!' said Becky.

'You are *kind*, Ermie,' said Sara. She laughed. 'It's magic, you know. When things are very bad, something nice always happens. Here we are, having a party!'

Ermengarde gave Sara and Becky some cake, and they began to eat. Suddenly, they stopped. There was a noise of feet on the stairs. They listened.

'Oh no!' whispered Becky. 'It's – it's Miss Minchin!'

'Yes,' said Sara. Her face was white again.

Then the door opened, and Miss Minchin came in.

'So, Lavinia was right,' she said angrily. 'Tea with Princess Sara! Becky, get back to your attic at once!'

'Tea with Princess Sara!' Miss Minchin said angrily.

31

'Oh, please, Miss Minchin!' cried Ermengarde. 'It was my cake, from home. We're only having a party.'

'Go back to your room, Ermengarde,' Miss Minchin said coldly, 'and take these things with you. And tomorrow' – she looked at Sara – 'there's no breakfast, no dinner, and no tea for you. Remember that!'

Soon the attics were quiet again. Tired and hungry, the two servant-girls went to sleep. But after an hour or two Sara opened her eyes. Was it a noise from the window perhaps?

'Something is different,' Sara whispered. 'What is it?' She sat up in bed and looked round the room. She looked again and again, and her eyes were very big.

The room *was* different – very different. There was a wonderful hot fire. There were new, warm blankets on her bed, and beautiful pictures on the walls.

Sara slowly got out of bed. 'Is this a dream?' she said. 'Where did all these things come from?' She put out her hand to the fire. 'No, it's not a dream. The fire is hot – I can feel it. And oh! Look at the table!'

There was a red cloth on the table, and cups and plates. There was hot tea, and wonderful things to eat – hot meat pies and sandwiches and cake, oranges and apples.

Sara ran to Becky's room. 'Becky,' she whispered. 'Come quickly. The magic is here again. Come and look.'

When Becky saw the room, she could not speak at first. Then she said, 'Oh, Miss! What is it? How did all these things get here?'

'I don't know,' said Sara. 'It's magic. At first I thought

On the table there were wonderful things to eat.

it was a dream, but it isn't. Look – these pies are hot. Let's eat them. Hot meat pies aren't a dream!'

They sat down by the fire, and ate and drank.

'Oh, those pies were good, Miss!' Becky said. 'And the tea and the cake. I don't understand magic, but I like it!'

Sara looked round the room. 'Oh, Becky, look! There are some books, too. I didn't see them before.'

She ran to look at them, and opened the top book. 'There's some writing here! Listen. It says, "To the little girl in the attic. From a friend." Oh, Becky!' Sara closed the book and looked up. 'I have a friend, Becky,' she said slowly. 'Someone is my friend.'

The next morning Becky met Sara in the kitchen.

'Oh, Miss,' she whispered. 'Was the magic there this morning? Or did it go away in the night?'

'No, it's still there,' Sara whispered back. 'I ate some cold meat pie for breakfast. And the fire was still warm!'

Becky laughed happily. 'Oh my! Oh my!' she said.

Miss Minchin could not understand it. When Sara came into the schoolroom, she looked happy and well. Miss Minchin wanted to see a white, unhappy face, and eyes red from crying. 'How can that child smile?' she thought angrily. But of course, she did not know about the magic.

And the magic did not go away. Every evening, when

'Was the magic there this morning?' Becky whispered.

Sara went up to bed, she found new things in the attic. There were more warm blankets, for her and for Becky. There were pictures on the walls; there were books, new shoes, and a winter coat. And best of all, there was always a fire, and a wonderful hot dinner on the table.

'But where does it all come from?' Becky said one night when they sat by the fire. 'Who does it, Miss?'

'A friend does it,' Sara said. 'A kind, wonderful friend. But he doesn't want us to know his name.'

They began to look at one of the new books, and then Becky looked up.

'Oh, Miss,' she whispered. 'There's something at the window. What is it?'

Sara got up to look. 'It's the monkey!' she said. 'The monkey from next door.' She opened the window, and the monkey jumped down into her arms. 'Oh, you poor little thing,' Sara said. 'You're so cold!'

Becky was very interested. 'I never saw a monkey before,' she said. 'He's not very beautiful, Miss! What are you going to do with him?'

'It's very late now,' said Sara. 'He can stay in my room tonight, and I can take him home in the morning.'

'Oh, you poor little thing,' Sara said.

6
Lost and found

◈ ◈ ◈

The next morning, the first visitor to the house next door was Mr Carmichael, back from Russia. But when he came into the house, his face was sad. Mr Carrisford knew the answer at once.

'You didn't find her,' he said.

'I found her,' Mr Carmichael said. 'But it was the wrong girl. Her name is Emily Carew, and she's much younger than Ralph Crewe's daughter. I'm very sorry.'

'We must begin again,' said Mr Carrisford unhappily. 'But where? It's two years now. Two years!'

'Well, she isn't at a school in Paris. We know that,' Mr Carmichael said. 'Let's look at schools in England now.'

'Yes,' said Mr Carrisford. 'Yes, we can begin in London. There's a school next door, Carmichael.'

Perhaps it was the magic again, but at that moment Ram Dass came quietly into the room.

'The little servant-girl from the attic is here,' he said to Mr Carrisford. 'With the monkey. He ran away again last night to her room. Would you like to see her?'

'Yes,' said Mr Carrisford. 'Yes, I would. Bring her in.'

And so Sara came into the room and stood in front of the Indian gentleman. She smiled at him.

'Your monkey came to my room last night,' she said, 'and I took him in because it was so cold.'

Mr Carrisford watched her face with interest. 'That was kind of you,' he said.

Sara looked at Ram Dass by the door. 'Shall I give him to the lascar?' she asked.

'I was born in India,' Sara said.

'How do you know he is a lascar?' said Mr Carrisford.

'Oh, I know lascars,' Sara said. 'I was born in India.'

Mr Carrisford sat up suddenly. 'In India?' he said. 'But you're a servant at the school next door.'

'Yes, I am now,' said Sara. 'But I wasn't at first.'

The Indian gentleman looked at Mr Carmichael, and then Mr Carmichael looked at Sara.

'What do you mean by "at first", child?' he asked.

'When Father first took me to the school.'

'Where is your father?' said Mr Carmichael.

'He died,' said Sara, very quietly. 'His friend ran away with all his money, and there was no money for me. There was nobody to take care of me. So Miss Minchin put me in the attic and said I must work for my bread.'

The Indian gentleman moved in his chair. 'What – what was your father's name?' he said. 'Tell me.'

Sara looked at him sadly. 'Ralph Crewe,' she said. 'He died in India from a fever, two years ago.'

Mr Carrisford's face went very white. 'Carmichael,' he whispered, 'it is the child – the child!'

That was an exciting day for many people. At first poor Sara did not understand. But Mr Carmichael talked to her quietly and told her everything – the true story about her father's friend and the diamond mines, and the two years of looking for Ralph Crewe's daughter.

'And all the time I was in the house next door.'

'And all the time,' she said later to Mr Carrisford, when they sat by his fire, 'I was in the house next door.'

Tom Carrisford took her hand. 'Yes,' he said. 'And you're never going back there. Your home is with me now. I'm going to take care of Ralph's Little Missus.'

Sara laughed, happily. 'And you were the friend, too. All those beautiful things in my attic came from you – you and Ram Dass. Becky and I thought it was magic!'

The Indian gentleman smiled at her. 'We were sorry for you,' he said. 'Ram Dass can move very quietly, and he carried the things across the roof when you were out. I couldn't find Ralph's daughter, but I wanted to help somebody. And then Ram Dass told me about this sad, lonely little servant-girl in the attic next door.'

And so the story ended happily for everybody – but not for Miss Minchin. Sara was very rich now, and Miss Minchin wanted her to come back to the school. She came to see Mr Carrisford, but he said some very angry things to her, and she went away with a red face.

Becky came to live in Mr Carrisford's house, too. She was Sara's servant, and she was very happy. She had a warm room, nice dresses, and good things to eat every day. And she loved Sara very much.

Ermengarde often came to visit Sara, and Sara helped her with her school lessons again. Ermengarde was not clever, but she was a true friend. On that first day in the Indian gentleman's house, Sara wrote a letter to her, and Ermengarde carried the letter into the schoolroom.

'There *were* diamond mines,' she told Lavinia and the other girls. 'There *were*! There were millions and millions of diamonds in the mines, and half of them are Sara's. And they were her diamonds all the time when she was cold and hungry in the attic. And she was a princess *then*, and she's a princess *now*!'

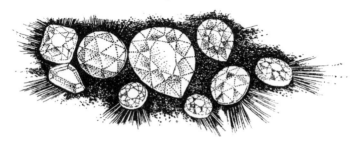

GLOSSARY

brave   not crying or asking for help when you are very unhappy

buy (past tense **bought**)   to give money to get something

clever   a clever person can learn, understand, and do things
  quickly and well

dream   a picture in your head when you are sleeping

fever   when you are ill with a very hot head and body, you have
  a fever

gentleman   a man of good family, often rich

hard   difficult; not easy

kind   friendly and good to other people

lascar   an Indian seaman

lawyer   a person who knows about the law

lonely   unhappy because you are not with other people

magic   when strange, exciting, unusual things happen

next door   the nearest house to your house

poor   you say 'poor' when you feel sad for somebody

princess   the daughter of a king or queen

sad   not happy

servant   a person who works in another person's house

take care of   to be kind to somebody; to give them love, a home,
  food, clothes, etc.

unhappy   not happy

whisper *(v)*   to speak very, very quietly

A Little Princess

ACTIVITIES

ACTIVITIES

Before Reading

1 **Read the back cover and the story introduction on the first page of the book. How much do you know now about the story? Tick one box for each sentence.**

	YES	NO
1 Sara Crewe is very rich.	☐	☐
2 Sara first comes to England when she is eleven years old.	☐	☐
3 Sara is a princess.	☐	☐
4 Miss Minchin likes little rich girls.	☐	☐
5 Sara is happy when her father leaves.	☐	☐
6 Everybody wants to be Sara's friend.	☐	☐

2 **What is going to happen in this story? Can you guess? Tick one box for each sentence.**

	YES	NO
1 Mr Crewe dies.	☐	☐
2 Mr Crewe goes to prison.	☐	☐
3 Mr Crewe loses all his money.	☐	☐
4 Sara is poor, hungry, and sad all her life.	☐	☐
5 Sara has no friends.	☐	☐
6 After a time Sara finds some new friends.	☐	☐
7 She runs away from Miss Minchin's school.	☐	☐
8 She goes back to India.	☐	☐

While Reading

Read Chapter 1, and then complete these sentences with the right words.

clever, expensive, lessons, like, princess, rich, richer, sad

1 Miss Minchin liked Sara because her father was _____.
2 Mr Crewe bought many _____ things for his daughter.
3 Miss Minchin thought Sara looked like a little _____.
4 When Mr Crewe left London, Sara was very _____.
5 Sara's friend Ermengarde was not _____, so Sara helped her with her school _____.
6 Sara's father was _____ than Lavinia's father, and because of that, Lavinia did not _____ Sara.

Read Chapter 2. Who said or wrote this, and to whom?

1 'My friend has some mines in northern India.'
2 'To me, you *are* a princess.'
3 'Sit down again for a minute. You look so tired.'
4 'Sometimes I like your stories better than things to eat.'
5 'Mr Crewe's good friend ran away with all Mr Crewe's money.'
6 'She must leave my school at once.'
7 '. . . you must be a servant and work for your bread.'

Before you read Chapter 3, can you guess the answer to this question?

Are any of these people going to be kind to Sara?

Miss Minchin / Ermengarde / Becky / Lavinia

Read Chapter 3. Are these sentences true (T) or false (F)? Change the false sentences into true ones.

1 Sara often cried in the first months of her new life.
2 She worked from early in the morning to late at night.
3 One morning Lavinia came up to her attic room.
4 Sara was very sad when Ermengarde came to see her.
5 Sara never saw anybody at the next attic window.
6 Then the Carmichael family came to live next door.

Read Chapter 4, and answer these questions.

Why

1 . . . did Ram Dass come across the roof to Sara's room?
2 . . . did Sara feel sorry for the Indian gentleman?
3 . . . did Mr Carrisford want to find Ralph Crewe's child?
4 . . . did Mr Carrisford run away from Ralph in India?
5 . . . was Mr Carrisford sorry for the little servant-girl next door?
6 . . . did Mr Carmichael go to Moscow?
7 . . . did Sara give her bread to a child in the street?
8 . . . was Sara very unhappy that night?

Before you read Chapter 5, can you guess what happens? Choose some of these answers.

1 Ram Dass goes to Sara's attic, but Sara doesn't see him.
2 Ram Dass leaves some money for Sara in her room.
3 Sara talks to Ram Dass and tells him her name.
4 Ram Dass tells Mr Carrisford that Sara is Ralph Crewe's daughter.
5 The monkey runs away again to Sara's room.

Read Chapters 5 and 6, and then join these halves of sentences together.

1 One night Ermengarde took a cake to Sara's room, . . .
2 Later that night Sara found some wonderful things in her room, . . .
3 Every evening after that, when Sara went to bed, . . .
4 Sara knew that she had a kind, wonderful friend, . . .
5 Then the monkey came to Sara's room one night, . . .
6 She talked about lascars and India and her father, . . .

7 and at first she and Becky thought it was magic.
8 and the next day Sara took him back to the Indian gentleman's house.
9 but Miss Minchin came up and stopped the party.
10 so Mr Carrisford found Ralph Crewe's daughter at last.
11 but she did not know his name.
12 there were new things in the attic for her and for Becky.

After Reading

1 **At the end of the story Sara wrote a letter to Ermengarde. Complete her letter with the words below. (Use one word for each gap.)**

after, better, care, diamonds, fever, find, friend, half, home, house, kind, know, live, mines, next, nicest, servant, wonderful

Dear Ermie,

I have something _____ to tell you! I am writing this in the Indian gentleman's _____. His name is Mr Carrisford, and he was my father's _____ in India. And, Ermie, there WERE _____ in the _____ – thousands of them – but they only found them _____ my father died.

  Mr Carrisford was ill with a _____ too, and when he got _____, he came to England to look for me. But he couldn't _____ me because he didn't _____ my name. And all the time, Ermie, I was a _____ in the house _____ door!

  _____ of the diamonds are mine now, Mr Carrisford says. But the _____ thing is this, Ermie. Mr Carrisford is a very _____ man, and he wants to take _____ of me. So I'm going to _____ with him and have a _____ again. You must come and visit me often.

  Your best friend, Sara

2 Here is a new illustration for the story. Find the best place in the story to put the picture, and answer these questions.

The picture goes on page _____.
1 Who is Sara talking to?
2 What is happening in Sara's room at this moment?
3 What happens next?

Now write a caption for the illustration.

Caption: _____

3 **How did Miss Minchin find out about Ermengarde's cake and the tea party in the attic? Put her conversation with Lavinia in the right order, and write in the speakers' names. Lavinia speaks first (number 5).**

1 _____ 'Upstairs, in the attic.'

2 _____ 'Yes, Lavinia, what is it?'

3 _____ 'A big cake. She said Sara was hungry.'

4 _____ 'Having tea with—! How do you know this, Lavinia?'

5 _____ 'Oh, Miss Minchin. I have something to tell you!'

6 _____ 'A box? What was in it?'

7 _____ 'She's having tea with Princess Sara.'

8 _____ 'Of course she isn't hungry! Right. I'm going upstairs at once. You were right to tell me this, Lavinia. You can go back to bed now.'

9 _____ 'I saw her on the stairs, with a big box.'

10 _____ 'But it's after ten o'clock! Where is she?'

11 _____ 'What's she doing up there?'

12 _____ 'Ermengarde isn't in her bed, Miss Minchin.'

4 **Here is Miss Minchin, telling someone about Sara. How many untrue things does she say? Can you correct them?**

'Sara Crewe? Oh yes, she lives across the street now, with Mr Carrisford, her father's brother. I was very kind to her when her father died in Africa. She slept in the best bedroom, and was never cold or hungry. She taught French to the younger children, but she didn't work in the kitchen or the house. I saw Mr Carrisford yesterday. He was very friendly, and he wants Sara to come back to my school.'

5 **Here is a puzzle. The answer is a word from the story with eight letters. To find the word, choose the right letters (one from each sentence) and write them in the boxes.**

At first there were lots of them; then there were none of them, but in the end there were lots of them. What are they?

☐ ☐ ☐ ☐ ☐ ☐ ☐ ☐

My first is in SAD.   My fifth is in COOK.
My second is in ILL.   My sixth is in KIND.
My third is in TEA.   My seventh is in DOLL.
My fourth is in MAGIC.   My eighth is in PRINCESS.

6 **What did you think about the people in this story? Choose some names, and finish these sentences in your own words.**

Sara / Ermengarde / Lavinia / Becky
Mr Crewe / Miss Minchin / Mr Carrisford / Ram Dass

1 I felt sorry for _____ because _____.
2 I liked _____ because _____.
3 I didn't like _____ because _____.
4 _____ was right to _____.
5 _____ was wrong to _____.

ABOUT THE AUTHOR

Frances Eliza Hodgson Burnett was born in Manchester, England, in 1849. When she was sixteen, her family went to the USA, and made their home in Knoxville, Tennessee. There, she began to write stories for magazines, because her family was poor and needed the money. She married in 1873, but went on writing, and her first novel, *That Lass o' Lowrie's*, came out in 1877. After that came more stories for adults and children, but in 1886 she wrote *Little Lord Fauntleroy*, and this book made her famous. Her next famous book was *Sara Crewe* (1888), and this came out as a longer story called *A Little Princess* in 1905. It was made into a film in 1939, with Shirley Temple as Sara, and another successful film came out in 1995. There has also been a television film of the story.

Both *Little Lord Fauntleroy* and *A Little Princess* are about very nice, good children. Many parents bought these books because they wanted their children to learn from the little lord and the 'little princess' how to be good. Today, most people think that *The Secret Garden* (1910) is Burnett's best book. In this story the children are more like real children – they are difficult, they get angry, they shout and they scream. There are many films of this famous and much-loved story.

Frances Hodgson Burnett was a very popular writer in her time. She often came back to visit England, but she died in the USA in 1924, in a beautiful house on Long Island.

OXFORD BOOKWORMS LIBRARY

Classics • Crime & Mystery • Factfiles • Fantasy & Horror
Human Interest • Playscripts • Thriller & Adventure
True Stories • World Stories

The OXFORD BOOKWORMS LIBRARY provides enjoyable reading in English, with a wide range of classic and modern fiction, non-fiction, and plays. It includes original and adapted texts in seven carefully graded language stages, which take learners from beginner to advanced level. An overview is given on the next pages.

All Stage 1 titles are available as audio recordings, as well as over eighty other titles from Starter to Stage 6. All Starters and many titles at Stages 1 to 4 are specially recommended for younger learners. Every Bookworm is illustrated, and Starters and Factfiles have full-colour illustrations.

The OXFORD BOOKWORMS LIBRARY also offers extensive support. Each book contains an introduction to the story, notes about the author, a glossary, and activities. Additional resources include tests and worksheets, and answers for these and for the activities in the books. There is advice on running a class library, using audio recordings, and the many ways of using Oxford Bookworms in reading programmes. Resource materials are available on the website <www.oup.com/elt/gradedreaders>.

The *Oxford Bookworms Collection* is a series for advanced learners. It consists of volumes of short stories by well-known authors, both classic and modern. Texts are not abridged or adapted in any way, but carefully selected to be accessible to the advanced student.

You can find details and a full list of titles in the *Oxford Bookworms Library Catalogue* and *Oxford English Language Teaching Catalogues*, and on the website <www.oup.com/elt/gradedreaders>.

THE OXFORD BOOKWORMS LIBRARY
GRADING AND SAMPLE EXTRACTS

STARTER • 250 HEADWORDS

present simple – present continuous – imperative –
can/cannot, must – *going to* (future) – simple gerunds …

Her phone is ringing – but where is it?

Sally gets out of bed and looks in her bag. No phone. She looks under the bed. No phone. Then she looks behind the door. There is her phone. Sally picks up her phone and answers it. *Sally's Phone*

STAGE 1 • 400 HEADWORDS

… past simple – coordination with *and, but, or* –
subordination with *before, after, when, because, so* …

I knew him in Persia. He was a famous builder and I worked with him there. For a time I was his friend, but not for long. When he came to Paris, I came after him – I wanted to watch him. He was a very clever, very dangerous man. *The Phantom of the Opera*

STAGE 2 • 700 HEADWORDS

… present perfect – *will* (future) – *(don't) have to, must not, could* –
comparison of adjectives – simple *if* clauses – past continuous –
tag questions – *ask/tell* + infinitive …

While I was writing these words in my diary, I decided what to do. I must try to escape. I shall try to get down the wall outside. The window is high above the ground, but I have to try. I shall take some of the gold with me – if I escape, perhaps it will be helpful later. *Dracula*

... should, may – present perfect continuous – *used to* – past perfect –
causative – relative clauses – indirect statements ...

Of course, it was most important that no one should see
Colin, Mary, or Dickon entering the secret garden. So Colin
gave orders to the gardeners that they must all keep away
from that part of the garden in future. ***The Secret Garden***

STAGE 4 • 1400 HEADWORDS

... past perfect continuous – passive (simple forms) –
would conditional clauses – indirect questions –
relatives with *where/when* – gerunds after prepositions/phrases ...

I was glad. Now Hyde could not show his face to the world
again. If he did, every honest man in London would be proud
to report him to the police. ***Dr Jekyll and Mr Hyde***

STAGE 5 • 1800 HEADWORDS

... future continuous – future perfect –
passive (modals, continuous forms) –
would have conditional clauses – modals + perfect infinitive ...

If he had spoken Estella's name, I would have hit him. I was so
angry with him, and so depressed about my future, that I could
not eat the breakfast. Instead I went straight to the old house.
Great Expectations

STAGE 6 • 2500 HEADWORDS

... passive (infinitives, gerunds) – advanced modal meanings –
clauses of concession, condition

When I stepped up to the piano, I was confident. It was as if I
knew that the prodigy side of me really did exist. And when I
started to play, I was so caught up in how lovely I looked that
I didn't worry how I would sound. ***The Joy Luck Club***

The Phantom of the Opera

JENNIFER BASSETT

It is 1880, in the Opera House in Paris. Everybody is talking about the Phantom of the Opera, the ghost that lives somewhere under the Opera House. The Phantom is a man in black clothes. He is a body without a head, he is a head without a body. He has a yellow face, he has no nose, he has black holes for eyes. Everybody is afraid of the Phantom – the singers, the dancers, the directors, the Stage workers . . .

But who has actually seen him?

Pocahontas

RETOLD BY TIM VICARY

A beautiful young Indian girl, and a brave Englishman. Black eyes, and blue eyes. A friendly smile, a laugh, a look of love . . . But this is North America in 1607, and love is not easy. The girl is the daughter of King Powhatan, and the Englishman is a white man. And the Indians of Virginia do not want the white men in their beautiful country.

This is the famous story of Pocahontas, and her love for the Englishman John Smith.